Always Dao

Always Dao

William Irwin

poems

道

SHANTI ARTS PUBLISHING
BRUNSWICK, MAINE 04011

Always Dao

Published by Shanti Arts Publishing

Cover and interior design
by Shanti Arts Designs

Shanti Arts LLC
Brunswick, Maine
www.shantiarts.com

Printed in the United States of America

ISBN: 978-1-956056-04-4 (softcover)
ISBN: 978-1-956056-11-2 (epub)

Library of Congress Control Number: 2021945682

Images

Cover
Artist Unknown, Landscape, c. 1875. Paint on paper mounted on cloth. Walters Art Museum, Baltimore, Maryland. WC PD

Page 15
Zhao Zhiqian, 19th century. Ink on paper. Honolulu Museum of Art. WC PD

Page 23
Ouyang Xiu, 1007–72. WC PD

Page 30
Chen Jiru (1558–1639). Ink on gold-flecked paper. Metropolitan Museum of Art, New York City. PD

Page 38
Tu Long (1542–1605). Ink on paper. Metropolitan Museum of Art, New York City. PD

Page 45
Wang Ao (1450–1524). Ink on patterned paper. Metropolitan Museum of Art, New York City. PD

Page 51
Ni Yuanlu (1593–1644). Ink on paper. Metropolitan Museum of Art, New York City. PD

Page 56
Qian Feng (1740–95). Ink on paper.
Walters Art Museum, Baltimore, Maryland.
WC PD

Page 63
Weng Tonghe (1830–1904). Ink on silver-flecked red paper. Metropolitan Museum of Art, New York City. PD

Page 69
Bada Shanren (Zhu Da) (1626–1705). Ink on paper. Metropolitan Museum of Art, New York City. PD

Page 73
Attributed to **Emperor Gaozong** (1107–87). Ink on paper. National Palace Museum, Shilin, Taipei, Taiwan. Wikimedia Commons PD

Page 81
Deng Shiru (18th century). Ink on paper. Private Collection. Wikimedia Commons PD

Page 89
Zhao Buzhi (1053–1110), Laozi Riding an Ox. Wikimedia Commons PD

PD: Public Domain
WC: Wikimedia Commons

道

always Dao

dead fish flow,
living salmon
swim upstream,
but only when
Dao does deem

steps

distance
from here
to eternity
shorter than
calamity
to serenity

directions

suffering
is inward
service
is outward

force or farce

do you play the jazz
or does it play you?
is flow in the dance
or in my head?
do we create
or discover the Dao?

joy

toddler
sprays hose
and delights
in moving
the world

pretty doomed

little lost duckling
in
parking lot puddle

unfortunate reality

infallible cartographers
of fictional worlds
map the way
you must walk

religion

collective
effervescence
of crowds
causes madness
among men

honest mouth

yellow teeth
tell truth

nun with ruler

she was
BIG for Jesus
small for kindness

contagion

scratch
leads to itch
cough
to cough
yawn
to yawn

captivator

without warning
trips no wire
into its grip
ambush desire

first car

bought a
gin mill
jalopy
off pal's
poppy

紅思種蕅三十本

蓮裳一兄大人屬

惟餘舊書一百車

集均之鉥 趙之謙

15

a wrong way

walking down
up escalator
of life
courting chaos
seeking strife

misspent youth

some of the
best times
I ever had
I can't remember,
or so I'm told

Margaritaville

calm as a clam
cause can't
feel who I am

common denominators

for even numbers
it's two
for odd problems
it's me

DIY

rock, rebellion, and love
sometimes you
reinvent the wheel
from below not above

different drummer

any instrument
is percussive
if you bang on it

hardwired hell

pain dealer
joy stealer
broke
before breaking
drunk
before drinking
stunk
before stinking
collecting
court dates
not accolades

recidivist

riddle me
enrage me
then they
have to
cage me

conversion of convenience

got arrested,
got God,
got out.
Jesus in jail
still,
no doubt.

all reals

she thought
I was a
non-player character
now I know
how it feels

worst part

from inertial bed
dawn hangs heavy
and forecasts dread

something

fear feels good
when ease is impossible

worrying

felt so bad
he couldn't stop

exercise

felt so good
he quit

bait and switch

I'm a fool
for this life
such a sucker
every time
seek a reason
find a rhyme

cigarette despair

sitting on the side of the road
legs in the traffic
bad crew cut and beater
things won't go your way
not a cigarette to spare

hypnic jerk

sleep twitch
signals sandman
to push you
off the cliff

value time

to enjoy
the present
invest in
the future

application

no guarantees
or necessities
vet it mo'
then
let it go

good news envelope

out-of-breath
as heartbeat matches
incomprehension
in genuine joy

rebirth

could dead wood
become
a live metaphor?

think outside the box

the metaphors we
live by
are the words
we'll die by
trying to say
something new

bore?

difference
between a
chore and task?
one can be done
with devotion.
need to ask?

if you're careful

there can be
a silver lining
in golden silence

簡啓多日不相見誠以區区見發

多曽灼艾无知體中如何来日脩偶

在家或能見之以中醫者常有頌

以俗工深可与之論攝也亦有闇事思

相見不宣　脩再拜　廿日

学正足下

messy mind

look past appearance
to see clutter
is in my head
not on my bed

fullness of being

branches touching sky
roots digging turf
just me and this tree
would be enough

creative imperative

conscious thoughts
aside
take the random for
a ride

confirmation

you can always find
what you're looking for
if
you don't let evidence
get in the way

scatter plot

those who look
too hard
at a pattern
are sure
to find
a cause

hard learned humility

prediction is for
fools
chaos, complexity
rules

palindrome

do you hold
the tenet
or
does the tenet
hold you?

pride balloon

fat checks
inflate a
thin man

ignorant

don't know what
you don't know:
one size
fits you
not all

musing

the voice inside
can sing off-key
in full throat

marking time

make your move
in a rut
or in a groove
marching toward
undone and incomplete
going nowhere
shuffling feet

missed the train

I'm better off.
sweet reframing?
or sour graping?

clean slate

sometimes sleep
washes worry away

bardic barista

made me a poem
to start the day
made you a coffee
to carry away

top that

nothing says joy
better than a balloon,
except a balloon that
says 'Joy' on it!

just do it

empirical, no miracle,
man-crushable Buddha
has no mandates
desires no devotion,
try it yourself
practice in motion

above us

more spirit than soma,
birds beat bodies
by flight

June's womb

fluid movement
in a warm air bath
of ease, no wound

prescription lenses

with
the will to believe
God hides
in plain sight

dew drop

maybe I'm amazed
at the way you're
moved by blades
of grass
across
a weedy lawn

誤教⋯夕⋯⋯得也別帖籍手

弁告⋯代研文

眉道人陳繼儒書於

含譽堂

start now

existence
is given
life
is chosen

let go

when
mind
opens
hands
receive

Gita

do your
duty,
do your
best,
let fate
take the
rest.
casting off
fruit of action
is addition
not subtraction.

fragile

a happy life
is yours
for the making
a loving heart
is hers
for the breaking

(un)romantic reasoning

in a subjunctive mood
she could love you

like the sun

you only love
the way
she makes you feel

complaining

deliriously
unhappy
when
she's not

codependent

blaming and
bemoaning,
her insanity
felt familiar
acceptable
even
appropriate

last to know

what was,
is not.
robbed of
my past
by her lies.

divorced

a not un-
pleasant
sadness
stole over
solitude

despair circle

can't forget
loop of
isolation
and regret,
dis-eased
dis-graced
re-placed,
upset

noisy head

life of defiance
and reliance
on wrong,
in silence
hear violence
my song

need a fix

self-deception
is
a great drug
until
you run out

recovery meeting

beautiful broken people
gather in their ugliness
inhaling hope
like cigarette smoke

More beer

favorite thing
to drink
was More.
loved to drink
More than family
More than friends
More than money
More than life.

recovery discovery

didn't write
the book
but already
know the story

prayer for freedom

may people pass peacefully
through my mind
unmolested and uncontested

rapper in recovery

hi, my name
is
Enmity
Anonymity
M&Mity
Eminemity

mental hygiene

brush your brain.
no one
wants to smell
your bad mood.

Daoist

can't dance
or drum
but hear
the rhythm
of the river
and
conform to the
shape of the sound

need a mind wipe

can't unsee a
bell,
mental drama
insane
hell

not a thong

wear the world
like a loose garment

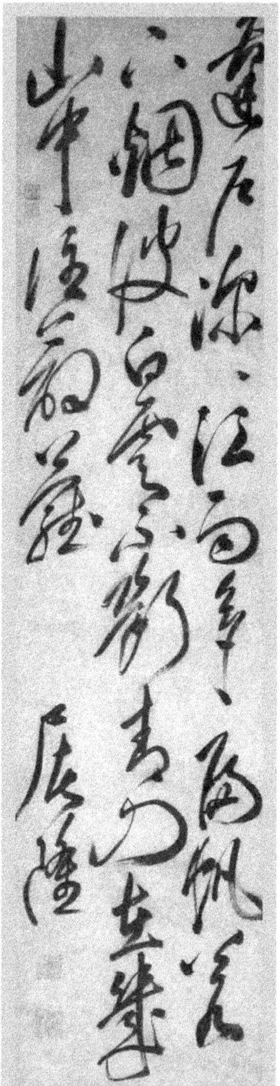

productive monotony

from the sanctuary
of sameness,
difference
breaks free

sun brain

blue sky
serotonin
high

dependency

toxins in
and
toxins out
the liver
of
the liver
must deliver
or
fall out

vice

inhabits me
in habits me

for yourself

do what is hard
until it's easy,
then do it not
to please me

boring benefits

excellence
takes
tolerance
to tedium
in training

habit's hammer

final strike
sunders stone
lightning gone
thunder alone

which is worse?

over
(thinking)
under

green and red

find flow
in action
and
inaction

e-motion

your feet
know the way
to feel better

chop wood

life inside
the mind
is enough
to make
you mad

forgotten flow

reality
leads to
humility
leads to
gratitude
leads to
happiness

no appreciation

for big
little things,
it's always
take-it-for-granted-Tuesday

appreciation

what if gratitude
was the gravity
that held things
in existence?

baby talk

fair is not
what you
say fair is

thought pollution

toxic sludge
from your brain
getting in my ear

sieve face

your character
leaks through
your mask

seen the light

radical change doesn't
make you right,
a certain uncertainty
would serve you tonight

paper clip bond

peerlessly plopped
pointlessly tangled
painfully separated

mismatch

was a good friend
but not good at
being my friend

but . .

a dead would
means nothing
to me now

think b4 U help

world is full
of people
who mean well
but do harm

無論歲書之

直源歲......又等

注妃後一......

活土珠而惘快......趣

榜......崴......

保......

謝......

才......士人書......

save yourself
a martyr declines
the oxygen mask
and
kills you
in the process

procreators
when
avoidamander
met
delayviator
procrastinator
was born
nine
monthslater

one thing
slave to
your inbox,
be a hedgehog
not a fox

brain programming

though with mouse in hand
I click and command,
this mind won't expand

Facebook fiend

habit havoc
dopamine slot machine
causes cortisol collapse

data addiction

how do you pay
the attention economy?

mind yourself

a placebo can work
even if you know
it's a placebo

nudge yourself

choose your choices
to avoid
your vices

choice architecture

free will is
more effective
when you need
less willpower

inside job

to rule
the world
influence
yourself

dream making

bend the world
to match my mind

attraction algorithm

the filter
is the secret,
program your mind
for what
you want to find

default

your fault
if
you accept
settings
and lies,
refuse to
customize

from yourself

happiness is
what happens
when you
look away

clear space

put it on
a Post-it
to take it
off mind

black and white

theories
and lenses
cleanse us
of gray vision,
can't see
with precision

speak not

iron sharpens iron
but
tempers sharpen tongues

faith in yourself

rational dreams
require
irrational beliefs

expand it

a world
awaits
between
stimulus
and
response

高舡如傑宅如篷
轂舳連牆去
船首北一睡未曾

兄堂筆署
送穉水郡新堂筆署
[印]

stoic mind

in control
of response
to what's
beyond control

mutant power

redefine,
labels only limit
if you let them

in a crowd

sing silently
at the top
of your voice

Judge Mental

finds you guilty
in the open court
of my closed mind

chatty Cathy

are you ever not talking,
morning woman
by my window walking?

don't be fooled

every
awesome dude
has an
asshole inside

neurotic authoritarian

his free-floating guilt
demands
symbolic gestures
from all

manic

off meds
or
on meth
anyway
out of mind

fell in

so busy
without doing anything
he could not mind the gap
between self-image and reality

the narcissist

he doesn't suffer from
delusions of grandeur
he enjoys them immensely

boss man

obnoxiously
overconfident
yet
refreshingly
incompetent

delusion of purpose

Shriner
directing traffic
in a parking lot

cock of the block

seriously
foolishly
officiously
friendly
little
mayor

slacker

no thriving force
able to lunch
not to launch

pre-resentment

already hate how I'm
anxiously anticipating
asinine antics from you

words words words

not dumb
not crazy,
his sentences
don't connect,
just lazy

溫之嵩山題字云蹬山有道

徐行則不困措足於平穩

之地則不跌戒之哉

豐

stormbringer

confluence clouds control,
another perfect storm?
maybe you play a role.

bright side

windbag in
Winnebago
at least
he leaves

and redundant

all she did
and said
was both
too little
and not
enough

like water

everything
is harder
in winter

mean god

cruel creator
wrought wrinkle
over
pimple crater

trip to top

making your way
in the world
2 steps at a time
up the down escalator
no need for rhyme

lukewarm

days of lots
days of little
both better
than middle

life is poker

seems like
skill when I win,
fortune when I fail.
where and why
does truth lie?

seriously absurd

if you're
not laughing,
you're
not looking

infernal Godot

abandon all hope
in what might
not never come

existential growth

you're a project
not an object
mindset not fixed
parts not broken
become yourself
not a token

holy

sures of black
and shades of white
a dead God haunts
my dreams tonight

forecast

plan but
don't project
anticipate
don't expect

moment of eternity

to slow time
stare at water

second noble truth

craving feeds craving
as salty snack
follows salty snack
long after hunger is satisfied
desire demands more suffering

consumed

craving,
compulsion,
I pop pralines
as one nut
feeds another

wired

high on my
own supply
of fear and
insecurity

misery maker

procrastination
seeks distraction
sans pleasure,
dishes to do
become treasure

toxic twins

arrogance and ignorance
lead the self-blind boy
quickly over the cliff

so long sobriety

did it
purposely
on accident,
when hard cider
sat near sweet tea,
one drink woke
the dragon,
now broke

tough fix

know where
in vein?
nowhere
in vain.

攤提盃觴
丙寅平旦
翁同龢

63

in jeopardy

pissing uphill
for the win

barstool boast

the change
that never
comes

unsober

halfway clean
is still dirty

subtle suicide

living to die
not dying to live

brain

the internal disquiet
combustion engine

creaks downstairs

fear of the basement,
unknown what lurks
in dusty corners of
subterranean mind

too much noise

who can spot
a black swan
when the sky is
falling
and the wolf
is at the door?

The Anxiety Express

freight train brain going nowhere
all night in a hurry

loser

no matter the outcome
results are insane
master debater
when I argue
in my brain

nunsense

penguins know magic
taught you to read
and add,
no reason to doubt
you'd go to Hell
if bad

reckoning REM

accountant's tricks
can't cheat sleep

realize

can't disguise
denial deep
in yellow eyes

drinking bubble

alone among others
selfishly cut off,
concealing my
dealing with death

gift of desperation

puts pride
on vacation
quickens quest
for restoration

dope sick gift

beautiful pain
delivers desperation,
detour from
death track and
final destination

rehab resolution

had a before life
will have an after life
then die embraced
by kids and wife

cluttered communication

sincere but not clear,
words can't express
when mind's a mess

stunning relief

how heavy
the load
didn't know
till lifted

内典以纸

之妃子甲寅以之賜山

書畫一具而先畫先一

嘉二の初也

西城先生

九月
卅五月

look again

paint removed
resembles
dirt added

butterfly

strain on skull
means brain's
breaking free

responsibility

stop looking
outside
for the enemy
within

saved by stupidity

burning bridges
in the rain

Dear Layne Staley

please color this dark world
with shades of melancholy
concealing spectra of despair

mindset

hope happens
when you decide
shit is fertilizer

scar display

pain has no claim
to your brain
deal and heal,
don't hide, the
suffering inside

apology allergy

can't say sorry?
try mea culpa

read the room

know the minds
by the bodies

stuck in a hurry

no spare change
this time
and can't
spare time
for this change

headache formula

complexity
without
justification

信使可覆　器欲難量　墨悲絲染
詩讚羔羊　景行維賢　剋念作聖
德建名立　形端表正　空谷傳聲　虛
堂習聽　禍因惡積　福緣善慶　尺

璧非寶　寸陰是競　資父事君
曰嚴與敬　孝當竭力　忠則盡命
臨深履薄　夙興溫凊　似蘭斯馨
如松之盛　川流不息　淵澄取映　容止

pre-filter

tone matters
for heards,
mind manners
with words

soft is hard

strength says
I can be kind
(even to you)

contrarian

don't be debunkinator,
pissing on parades.
be appreciator,
heaping accolades.

aesthetic challenge

sing don't censor,
find imperfections
that aren't flaws

wish well

need to love
people
I don't like

seeing anew

moon at noon
trees at night
outlines
spark delight

new eyes

consider
the strangeness
of a tree

dead and forgotten

lucky life isn't fair
got what I deserve
none would care

relief

cop car's lights
in the rearview
but not for me

say thanks

don't tell help
how to help

in my mind

all thoughts
allowed
some thoughts
unwelcome

lament less

the unlooked for
award
is never missed

restart the day

too early
to be
so sore
and surly

wu wei

don't try,
to win
a staring
contest
with
the sky

in ashes

sad but
not unhappy
sensed something
still inside

baptism

arise in ashes
from flame
become new

stranger

people are
so other
takes time
to tell them
you're brother

kinds of compathy

same shoes
sympathy
your shoes
empathy

confessin'

I'm too dumb
to get a blessin'
without feelin'
pain of lesson

10% happier

the voice in my head
is
a recovering asshole

awareness

minimize
mind
movement

doing nothing

sit on
your asana
to keep
moving still

meditation

doing nothing
without trying
takes practice

nothing more

trying to meditate
is
practicing meditation

white noise

waves of sound
drown me
into dreams

美德韶金石

君理有詩書

颖伯山民鄧

石如

virtual realities

worlds where I was,
lost.
as I tumble from bed,
dreams flee my head.

alarm clock evaluation

just fine
woke on time,
slept in segments
sewn together,
made a knight
to face the weather

true abundance

when there is
plenty in mind
then there is
plenty in pocket

Kondo mind

uncluttered thoughts
spark joy
with simple words

outgrowth

serve yourself
by serving others

gift

the shell has no surprise,
but the green delight
of the pistachio
brings joy with
every opening

Rhiannon

her love
is a gazebo
in the rain

after the fall
love
is living
without
excitement

wordless couples
we sit in quiet
saying nothing
never unease,
they sit in silence
saying nothing
discomfort dis-ease

things that should not be
poems without purpose
windows without view
thoughts without permission
memories without you

action
so much falsity,
so lead with love to
be the truth you believe

om

contagious calm
cures
contaminating concern

intrusive thoughts

prohibited pink pandas persist,
but when we wave
unwelcome white wolves walk
away

tree joy

eyes can't count
branches above
swallowing skies
sublime to love

war story

walked away
from a fight
to embrace
existence
and win

fire gaze

how long
can now
last before
thought
breaks
fragile
moment
with future
or past?

recipe

ego less
love more

no pressure

treasure of leisure
true pleasure
beyond measure

never free

Catholic atheist
sticky inside
like clean
Coke can

random happens

some seeds
plant themselves
don't mistake
order for design

life is Tetris

ain't jigsaw,
puzzle pieces
fall from sky
no single solution
to the open eye

time flow

forever comes
a day at a time
when you're
not looking

carefully

spend time
like it's money
spend money
like it's time

constant

unstable skies
make us realize
what's best,
even change
needs a rest

瞬瞬西由打失心情爾我誰
衝騎牛覓牛甚可著慎
子世方収立眷心眼腰直
竟勾未雜扎逞濃樂心誰
我之立我眉之修之 晉鄉

don't overlook

the happiness
of
deflated balloons,
petered out
and pleased
to
have purposed

educated palate

connoisseur
of life
tastes bitter
chocolate
in strife

no one listening

great acoustics
made peace
with the void
possible

for Camus

in the face
of the world's
gentle indifference
put a warm blanket
on your feet

shadow selves

people missed
before goodbyes
as they fade
in front of eyes

life sentence

death is
inevitable
dying is
optional

prison break

Socrates in fetter
Buddha knew better

mourning warning

stay out of cemeteries
that smother the dead
breathe in outfields
oxygen to your head

roam

many roads
lead to
big tent,
look back
at narrow way
wonder where
it went

reaper

Goldengrove's
ghost guessed
grim guest

life

a puzzle
with no answer
but many solutions

joy and suffering

the flower
opens outward
the ego
closes inward

love impart

do not depart
a life apart

atman and Brahman

will my wall
ever fall?
can we
join you
with me?

like this poem

life is short
but long enough

Odyssey

a poem is sent out
to a publisher
but comes home
to a reader

crickets

soundtrack for
a life
of
no applause

William Irwin is Professor of
Philosophy at King's College in
Pennsylvania, where he teaches
a course on Eastern Philosophy.
Irwin originated the philosophy
and popular culture genre of books
with *Seinfeld and Philosophy* in
1999. *The Simpsons and Philosophy*,
The Matrix and Philosophy, and
many other books followed. He
is the author of the novel *Little
Siddhartha: A Sequel* and has
published a poetry collection titled
Both/And.

SHANTI ARTS

NATURE · ART · SPIRIT

Please visit us online
to browse our entire book catalog,
including poetry collections and fiction,
books on travel, nature, healing, art,
photography, and more.

Also take a look at our highly
regarded art and literary journal,
Still Point Arts Quarterly, which
may be downloaded for free.

www.shantiarts.com

www.ingramcontent.com/pod-product-compliance
Lightning Source LLC
Chambersburg PA
CBHW021936040426
42448CB00008B/1096

* 9 7 8 1 9 5 6 0 5 6 0 4 4 *